THE DEACON AT WORK

Other books of interest:

The Deacon in a Changing Church	Donald F. Thomas
The Work of the Church Treasurer	Thomas E. McLeod
The Work of the Church Trustee	Orlando L. Tibbetts
The Work of the Church: Getting the Job Done in Boards and Committees	David Sawyer
The Work of the Clerk	Zelotes Grennell and Agnes Goss
The Work of the Deacon and Deaconess	Harold Nichols
The Work of the Pastoral Relations Committee	Emmett V. Johnson
The Work of the Usher	Alvin D. Johnson

THE
DEACON AT WORK

By FREDERICK A. AGAR

Author of

"A Manual of Church Methods," "The Stewardship of Life.
"Modern Money Methods for the Church," etc.

JUDSON PRESS ®

VALLEY FORGE

Copyright, 1923, by
GILBERT N. BRINK, Secretary

———

Published July, 1923

———

Twenty-eighth Printing, 1990
International Standard Book No. 0-8170-0783-0

———

Judson Press

Valley Forge, PA 19481

The name JUDSON PRESS is registered as a trademark in
the U.S. Patent Office.

Printed in U.S.A.

INTRODUCTION

Now there went with him great multitudes: and he turned, and said unto them, If any man cometh unto me, and hateth not his own father, and mother, and wife, and children, and brethren, and sisters, yea, and his own life also, he cannot be my disciple. Whosoever doth not bear his own cross, and come after me, cannot be my disciple. For which of you, desiring to build a tower, doth not first sit down and count the cost, whether he have wherewith to complete it? Lest haply, when he hath laid a foundation, and is not able to finish, all that behold begin to mock him, saying, This man began to build, and was not able to finish. Or what king, as he goeth to encounter another king in war, will not sit down first and take counsel whether he is able with ten thousand to meet him that cometh against him with twenty thousand? Or else, while the other is yet a great way off, he sendeth an ambassage, and asketh conditions of peace. So therefore whosoever he be of you that renounceth not all that he hath, he cannot be my disciple.—*Luke 14 : 25-33.*

INTRODUCTION

The local church needs to develop a Scriptural type of discipleship. Far too many members are names only on the church-membership roll. All the non-participants need special attention, and the only hope that it will be given to them lies in the development of lay officials competent, because trained, to lead the people aright.

This volume undertakes to set forth quite fully the opportunities and responsibilities that belong to the diaconate in the hope that the ministry will use it to train and develop, in every local church, deacons and deaconesses equipped to fill their office with success so that the Lord and Master may be honored in the deeds of all his servants.

FREDERICK A. AGAR.

NEW YORK CITY, APRIL, 1923.

CONTENTS

CHAPTER I

SCRIPTURE AND COMMON SENSE

1. Authority of Word

The authority of the Word of God is supreme with a Christian and with the local church in all its beliefs and practises.

The Scriptures are to be the basis upon which the local church is formed and upon which its membership is built up in the holy faith. The Word of God has the witness of the Spirit as to its truth and power, and therefore its authority must be recognized and upheld in a marked manner by all who compose the church and especially by its leaders, lay and professional.

2. Authority of Under-shepherd

The authority of the minister is personal and not ecclesiastical. It is primarily the authority of the Word of Truth and not man-made or delegated by an organized group. A minister's influence or authority is largely determined by his personal character and his Christian ability. For him to presume to give orders to the deacons or deaconesses is to presume to have a right which he does not and cannot possess. He is a personal leader at work for the Lord in a local church. His call to the pastorate of a local church does, however, also give him delegated authority from that body.

3. Scripture and Common Sense

Scripture and common sense are not in opposition but work out to the will of God when common sense is working along right lines. Common sense, to be what its name implies, must always be based upon the general teachings of the Word of God and must not be in opposition either to a specific teaching or to the trend of the general teachings of the Word. To illustrate the use of common sense here referred to, Scriptural teaching does not specifically state the number of deacons to be elected by a local church, hence that body should elect as many as are needed to maintain the organization upon its highest basis of efficiency. When that is done the Word of God and common sense working together have produced the needed result. The common sense of a Christian will never violate or override the revealed will of God as found in the Bible.

4. Common Sense

Common sense is the application of clear and right thinking to the underlying principles and consequent actions of life.

5. Extra-Biblical Machinery

Scripture teaches and leads by direction, and also by indirection. For instance, there is no specific command to produce an efficient church, but from many directions we have statements that would lead any careful reader to the knowledge that the God of all our mercies is expecting us to do a worth-while piece of work. It is therefore wise and proper for the local churches to build a simple and effective piece of machinery so that all the membership may find a place to worship, serve, and give. To do this a departmental organization seems wise, and the local church brings into action officials such as Bible school superintendent, Women's Union president, etc. These officials are in reality aids to the deacons and deaconesses, but there is no direct authority in the Bible for such offices; they are extra-Biblical. No sane person, however, would say that they were contrary either to the word or spirit of Scriptural teaching.

6. Life a Unit

" That the man of God may be thoroughly furnished unto every good work." The program of the local church must encompass as far as possible all that is needed to produce a well-rounded life. To presume that a church can minister to the soul side of man and disregard the life, is to depart from the Word of the Lord and also from common sense. An individual in the church must be faced by a plan which relates itself to his experience through a worked-out program that meets the needs of the whole life. Spiritual life is revealed in commercial circles as well as in the church edifice, and a Christian life finds expression both in the prayer-meeting and in the realms of social relaxation. One cannot be a Christian in the local church life and a selfish brute in the home circle. To attempt to build a superstructure of spiritual expression upon a foundation that is unchristian is to build a house upon the sands, for the storms and experiences of life will wreck it. The man, the whole man anywhere, everywhere, must in intent and purpose be seeking the way and will of God.

7. The Church

It is quite evident that the intention of the Founder of the local church was to have his institution occupy a central place in the social structure of humanity, because right social bases can only be produced upon a Christian foundation.

As an institution the local church was to be organized upon a most simple basis. Christ himself was to be the invisible head of the church universal and also of the local church. Under his leadership in the person of the Holy Spirit, an under-shepherd was to be sustained by the local body as a visible leader. He was to be assisted by deacons and deaconesses. Thus the Christian democracy was to produce a fraternity and ministry simple and effective because its whole fabric was founded upon love and equality. Whatever success the church has attained has been due to the production of the fraternal ministries which Christ's love alone can produce. Whatever failure has come to the church has been caused by the inability to produce a worth-while body of trained lay workers called deacons and deaconesses who, living with the remainder of the people, should lead them to love one another in a conspicuous and sacrificial Christian manner. Deacons and deaconesses can never attain to their rightful position until they have been clinically prepared by the Lord's servant called a pastor, who is commanded to be " apt to teach."

8. The Minister

The under-shepherd or pastor is not the servant of the board of deacons. The lay officers are not called to their office to run the preacher. Nor is the pastor the boss of the board of deacons. The minister is the leader of the church forces and he is to fill his place of leadership because he is a master in fulfilling all that is required to produce a church at work, at worship, and at all the tasks of stewardship.

The pastor is to teach and train the other church officers, and he cannot do that most important piece of work if his position of leadership is not assured in the eyes of every one and constantly used in the life of the church.

A church recently visited had a board of deacons who made the minister their tool and dependent. He was not allowed to attend the meetings of the deacons but was occasionally invited in when they desired his presence. They issued him orders about the conduct of his ministerial office and even laid out for him, without consultation, a series of sermons they commanded him to preach. Deacons who act in that manner are not fit for the office they occupy, but the pastor in turn showed incompetency, either because he accepted a church where such practises obtained or because, after having accepted the charge, he failed to assert his right to the place of leadership in all the concerns of the local church. The minister should be ex-officio a member of every board and committee in the church and should be the chairman of the board of deacons with a lay chairman as assistant.

9. The Bible and Deacons

" Likewise must the deacons be grave, not double-tongued, not given to much wine, not greedy of filthy lucre; holding the mystery of the faith in a pure conscience. And let these also be proved, then let them use the office of a deacon being found blameless.

" Let the deacons be the husbands of one wife, ruling their children and their own houses well. For they that have used the office of a deacon well, purchase to themselves a good degree, and great boldness in the faith which is in Christ Jesus " (1 Tim. 3 : 8-13).

" The powers that be are ordained of God " (Rom. 13 : 1).

" Render therefore to all their dues, honor to whom honor " (Rom. 13 : 7).

" And the things that thou hast heard of me among many witnesses, the same commit thou to faithful men, who shall be able to teach others also " (2 Tim. 2 : 2).

10. The Bible and Deaconesses

" Even so must women (deacons-deaconesses) be grave, not slanderers, sober, faithful in all things " (1 Tim. 3 : 11).

" I commend unto you Phœbe our sister which is a deaconess of the church which is at Cenchrea, that ye receive her in the Lord as becometh saints, and that ye assist her in whatsoever business she hath need of you, for she hath been a succorer of many and of myself also. Greet Priscilla and Aquila my helpers in Christ Jesus " (Rom. 16 : 1, 2).

11. Junior Deacons

Very distinctly the Word of the Lord indicates that the deacons are not to be hastily chosen, but that the office is to be filled by tried and proved men. " And let these also first be proved " (1 Tim. 3 : 10).

It would seem therefore within the spirit, if not within the letter, of revealed truth to have a school of training for the diaconate, as in olden times there was a school of the prophets where young men were taught and trained by the proved and experienced prophets.

Many churches have found it eminently practical to have a junior diaconate constituted under the authority of the church, in which group were young men chosen with an eye to the future needs of the church. Too often local churches have hastily selected untried and untrained men, and immediately after their election their unfitness for the office has been revealed; but it was next door to impossible to get rid of the unfit material, and trouble and inefficiency followed. There is no direct warrant in the Bible for a board of junior deacons, but on the other hand there is nothing in Scripture that would prevent a church from adopting such a common sense method of proving the personnel of a future diaconate.

12. Not Deacons

A careful reading of Acts 6 : 1-8 would seem to give no basis for the general belief that therein is found an account of the first election of deacons. The seven here selected were specifically detailed to perform merely the mechanical and secondary task of distributing to the needs of widows, while the spiritual ministrations of the Word were to be continued by the apostles in the spirit of prayer without the interruptions of such a distribution. It must be noted that

B

the inspired record in other places gives very vivid details of a much larger service rendered by some among the seven, in particular Philip and Stephen. Some one has suggested that this committee of seven was similar to some of the Hoover committees which distributed relief during the war. For the use of the reader the passage of Scripture is reprinted here in full:

And in those days, when the number of the disciples was multiplied, there arose a murmuring of the Grecians against the Hebrews, because their widows were neglected in the daily ministration. Then the twelve called the multitude of the disciples unto them, and said, It is not reason that we should leave the word of God, and serve tables. Wherefore, brethren, look ye out among you seven men of honest report, full of the Holy Ghost and wisdom, whom we may appoint over this business. But we will give ourselves continually to prayer, and to the ministry of the word. And the saying pleased the whole multitude: and they chose Stephen, a man full of faith and of the Holy Ghost, and Philip, and Prochorus, and Nicanor, and Timon, and Parmenas, and Nicolas a proselyte of Antioch: whom they set before the apostles: and when they had prayed, they laid their hands on them.

And the word of God increased; and the number of the disciples multiplied in Jerusalem greatly; and a great company of the priests were obedient to the faith. And Stephen, full of faith and power, did great wonders and miracles among the people.

If this is the record of the election of the first deacons, nothing in it is found to compel the local church to limit the number of deacons to seven or to have an "ordination" such as was used by the apostles in setting apart the seven to care for the neglected widows.

The activities of Stephen as recorded in verse eight are entirely beyond the scope and purpose of the appointment as recorded in verses 1-3 and therefore cause me to think that he was also a deacon.

13. "Husband of One Wife"

This statement has been wrongly interpreted and needs to be cleared up in the thinking of many churches. The inspired writer was living in a day when in many countries to which the gospel had been taken it was the custom for men to have several wives. This was not in accord with the law of Christ, so the apostle clearly defines that a deacon, if married, shall be the husband of but one wife. To make an unmarried man ineligible to the office of deacon is to misapply the statement and prevent some very fine Christian men from serving the Lord and the church.

14. Church Officers

The Bible gives some specific directions concerning pastors or under-shepherds and also about deacons and deaconesses. But it is not contrary to Scripture to elect and use such other officers as may be needed to produce a local church which does its work " decently and in order." Such other officers should not be considered inferior to the deacons or deaconesses, and any assumption of superiority on the part of deacons or deaconesses over other duly elected church officials is an evidence of unfitness for official duties. Common sense supports the Bible in its desire to produce an efficient instrument for righteousness. When therefore the spirit of truth prevails, a church is at liberty to appoint needed officials without any specific statement to support the particular officer needed by the demands of the work. On the other hand, the spirit of truth does not support pride, vainglory, or official arrogance. Nor will it permit such a multiplication of church officials as will tend to confusion and weakness. Scripture must be used in a common-sense way.

15. Tenure of Office

It has been the practise of many churches to elect deacons for life, and the general result has been to favor inefficiency and to promote incapacity. A limited tenure of office is best, say three or at the most five years. Scripture has no direction concerning this specific matter, so it is left for us to use our best judgment in order to produce a worth-while result. The life-tenure has produced some very curious results. For instance, a local church elected a deacon for life.

About seven years later the man moved to another city and caused the clerk to put a footnote on his church letter saying that he was a deacon. When the new church received the man by letter he demanded to be recognized as a deacon because the other democracy had elected him a deacon for life. He was much incensed when it refused to do so. It would be just as sensible for the president of the Brazilian democracy to come and live as a citizen in the United States and, because he had been elected to the presidency of Brazil, demand that he be recognized as our president. Unless the act of one local church receives the formal recognition of another local church, it has no bearing. This is illustrated in the ordination of a minister: another church recognizes the act of the ordaining church when it calls the man to be their pastor. The so-called ordination of deacons is a dangerous practise because it leads many people to wrong conclusions concerning the import of a setting-apart service. Today many churches have found it wise to limit the tenure of a deacon's term of office and then prescribe that he is not eligible to succeed himself until one year has elapsed, and this plan is commended because it prevents the formation of an official clique and tends to promote democracy and efficiency, which two elements are essential in a successful local church.

16. Deacon Stephen

Stephen was one of the seven whose election
is recorded in Acts 6 : 1-8. Concerning his work
it is written, " And Stephen, full of faith and
power, did great wonders and miracles among the
people " (Acts 6 : 8).

He preached the gospel of Jesus to the people
and rebuked them, as recorded in Acts 7, and
his sacrificial end is recorded in verses 59 and 60
of that chapter: " And they stoned Stephen, calling upon God and saying, Lord Jesus, receive
my spirit. And he kneeled down and cried with
a loud voice, Lord, lay not this sin to their
charge. And when he had said this, he fell
asleep."

If the seven were deacons, this record concerning Stephen sets a high standard for the modern
diaconate, but in any case it is a call to modern
Christian service and heroism.

17. Seven Deacons

A church should have deacons and deaconesses
in sufficient number to do the required work of
the local body. It is common sense that a church
of a thousand members needs a larger number
of lay officers than one with half that number of
members. Even if Acts 6 : 1-8 refers to deacons,
the fact that seven was the number there is no
indication that such a number was the will of the

Lord elsewhere unless there is an explicit statement to that effect. No such limitation as to the number of deacons is set forth there, so a local church may select and train enough men and women to do the work required by the local situation.

18. Women Officials

In all the years during which the history of the local churches has been in the making women have furnished much of the service and power of its spiritual life and lay ministry.

Long ago Paul wrote a specific statement to a specific church with some internal trouble caused by foolish women. To permit that statement to prevent all women from using their God-given endowments is to be blind to other teachings by the same and other writers upon the same topic. It is also a perversion of fact when the evident blessing of God rests today upon the utterances and services of multitudes of the best servants that our Lord possesses in the local churches. This is the testimony of present-day experience. To prevent women from speaking in the church, and then allow them to sing in the choir of that same church and to teach in a part of the whole church called the Bible school, presents one of those curious but danger ous mental twists that belong only with a warped or prejudiced mind.

To pin a practise irrevocably to a statement made under the specific facing of the difficulties in one local church and then to apply that specific statement to all churches, whether or not the troublesome conditions exist in them, is not a good exhibition of Christianity or of logic. To exclude women everywhere because one church in the experience of an apostle had troublesome women, is to harm the cause of the kingdom. Paul applied other statements to specific conditions. Why not use the same logic and, for instance, force every church-member to greet the others with a kiss? Paul directed in one of his letters how a woman was to dress when she prayed or prophesied, and evidently referred to public speech. The church needs women officials to share its burdens with men, and in the light of modern Christian experience the blessing of the Lord rests upon the words and works of women as they serve God in the local church. Every local church should have women officials called deaconesses.

19. Deaconesses

For many years the local church has suffered seriously from an unchristian prejudice against women and has made sex distinctions that are unwise and harmful. The Scriptures make plain the fact that there is no sex discrimination regarding spiritual functions, for the promises and powers of God are to every one alike, as Paul makes plain in Galatians 3 : 28. Paul's much discussed remark concerning disorderly women who spoke with tongues as found in 1 Corinthians 14 : 34 did not prevent him from recognizing the office of deacons, recording even the names of some deaconesses, Phœbe for instance, in the early church. Then in another place (1 Cor. 11 : 5) he gave directions about how a woman should dress when she prayed or prophesied in the church. Inasmuch as the modern local church is composed of an average of sixty-five per cent. of females, common sense would dictate the use of women officials whose specific duty would be the care of the female members. In another place the specific duties of the deaconess are thoroughly discussed.[1]

20. Deacon's Wives

In 1 Timothy 3 : 11 the King James translation makes Paul say, " Even so *must their* wives be grave, not slanderers, sober, faithful in all things." This translation is wrong and dangerously misleading, for it would constitute the wife of a deacon, *per se*, an official of the local church. The spirit of God would not allow such a dangerous statement to be the inspired teaching in that respect. For instance, in a church where I was

[1] See R. B. C. Howell, " The Deaconship." The teaching in Section 19 above accords with the view of an eminent Southern authority as found in Mr. Howell's book.

pastor there was a very fine Christian man on
the board of deacons. He was a conspicuous
example of an efficient spiritual officer. His wife
was a member of the church and a constant attendant, but she had a tongue which she would
not control and which was constantly stirring up
troubles in the congregation. If, because she was
the wife of a deacon, she had had official status,
the resultant damage would have wrecked the
church, as a board of deaconesses is constantly
called upon to act in cases of great importance
where secrecy is one of the prime requisites. On
the other hand, to deprive the man of his office
and the church of the services of such a capable
official would have worked serious injury to the
cause. The inspired Word is correct, but the
King James translators made an erroneous translation. Deacons' wives should have no official
status unless selected for an office by a vote of
the local democracy.

21. Precedents—Custom

Many a church is governed in its action by
"what has been," by precedents and customs,
regardless of whether or not the Word of God
has been followed and common sense has dictated
the past procedures. If a certain line of action
is in accord with the Word of the Lord, it can be
made to produce the desired result if the people
will use their inherent powers under the leader-

ship of the Spirit of God. But when, without
warrant of Scriptures, a failure is perpetuated
upon the basis of "We have always done it that
way," then one is inclined to decide that selfish-
ness and ease are at the root of the matter, or
else that people love their own way more than
the will and way of God. Situations exist all
over our land where local churches are condemned to failure and inefficiency because of
custom and precedents which are without any
Scriptural foundations.

The number of deacons in a church should be
doubled or trebled when necessary, and deaconesses might well be appointed to fulfil their Scriptural office. The deacons will welcome training
for their official duties, in spite of precedents or
customs of bygone days.

22. Idealism

Very often people are heard to remark, "Oh
yes, he is an idealist," as though idealism was
impractical and a reproach. Jesus was an idealist, and every one who undertakes to follow him
must be an idealist in word and deed. Idealism
is the goal of every Christian, and his sense and
sanity are revealed as he aims high and constantly attempts to produce the highest and best
results obtainable in his own life and in the life
of the divine institution called the local church.
Not to be an idealist in spirit and purpose is to

depart from the aims which our Lord Christ set before us. Idealism is Scriptural and full of common sense in all its outreach.

Questions

1. What is the basis upon which a local church is to be instituted?

2. Give a definition of common sense and relate it to Scriptural teaching.

3. To what part of life does the gospel apply? Quote the verse of Scripture applicable to the answer to this question.

4. Quote the Scriptural verses which directly concern the office of deacon.

5. Make an analysis of Acts 6 : 1-8.

6. What is said about the term of service for a deacon? Give the reasons for your answer.

7. Quote the King James translation of 1 Timothy 3 : 11 and discuss it from the standpoint of common sense.

8. Upon what basis should church practises be maintained? Why are some customs or precedents dangerous?

CHAPTER II

SELECTING AND NEED OF TRAINING

23. Selecting Officers

Great care should be taken in the selection of people for such an important office as deacon or deaconess. If a regular training-council is held the local church will have a wider field from which to choose officials, as many people not now competent can easily be trained into competency for an official position.

After a careful survey of the membership by a competent nominating committee, selection should be made, and after election the processes of training should immediately proceed under the guidance of the pastor.

It must always be remembered that the person selected to fill the Scriptural office of deacon is not inducted into an order, but is merely elected to fill an office during the pleasure of a democracy.

24. Untrained Officiary

When real consideration is given to the failure of the local church forces to prepare and train a lay officiary by clinical methods, the wonder is how the church has been able to accomplish what it has in the past. Surely it is an evidence of its divine origin. What marvelous things might have been wrought if the untrained, groping, and often bewildered officials had known what to do and how to do it.

25. The Up-and-Down Church

Church after church has had an active pastor under whose leadership progress had been made. Then came the day when the pastor departed, and within a short time all the progress had disappeared and the church was away down at the bottom of the ladder of progress. Another pastor came along, and it took months and years to regain the ground lost between the going of one and the coming of another minister. Why? One reason was the failure to train a group of lay leaders to do the task of maintaining a working church for, without the pastor, there was no inherent capacity for holding the church to a good level of living and working.

A certain pastor through seven years of leadership trained and developed a corps of capable officials. After he left that pastorate the lay leaders for more than a year continued the high standard of service and productivity of former days, so that when finally the new pastor came he found a spirit of progress and a desire for even larger productiveness. Such work by any pastor constitutes the highest form of honor to the reputation of the ministry.

26. A Day of Specialization

This is a time of specialization, and the church needs as much if not more than any other organization to use the specialist, because its work is vital to the welfare of individuals and the world and to the saving of a world of lost souls.

The Bible-school work in the local church has been developed so that the officers and teachers are specialists, more or less, in the work they are doing.

It is common sense that the diaconate shall become a group of specialists so that they may do the work of their office on a high plane. Educational methods which will include clinical training must be used to develop the deacons and deaconesses until they are recognized in their local spheres as special workers worthy of honor and emulation.

27. Training Deacons

Every local church should require the deacons or deaconesses to attend a course of training conducted each year by the pastor. The pastor is the normal person to conduct such a clinic. A regiment is strong and dynamic because it has a succession of trained officers for all its component parts. Without trained officers the regiment would be a mob, unwieldy and dangerous. The average church is a mob with a pastor trying to bring order and discipline into the midst of a group of undisciplined people.

If the pastor is not competent to train the deacons he is not capable of filling his office. If the diaconate refuse to be trained to know and do their work, they are not fitted for the work to which the church has called them. It is admitted that many a pastor will have a somewhat difficult task to start the needed training-class because of past conditions, but a season of earnest prayer will so change those conditions in most

cases that the training-class can be established
and good will result. In some cases it might be
wise to invite a neighboring pastor to start the
class, particularly where certain personalities
bulk large and some drastic changes must be
wrought out. But a trained lay officiary must be
produced as quickly as possible, and the difficulties in the path must be made the incentives to
the accomplishment of a real piece of work to
strengthen the local church as an instrument to
be used of the Lord.

28. Church Training-Council

After every election of officers in the local
church, the pastor should organize and conduct a
church officers' training-council, one section of
which should be for deacons and deaconesses. If
the church conducts an annual church school, the
training-course may well be made a part of its
work; but if no such school is held, then four sessions of an hour apiece should be planned to precede or follow the midweek prayer-service for
four successive weeks each year.

The newly elected officiary should all be expected to qualify for their official duties by attendance upon the council.

29. City Training-Council

Great difficulty is sometimes experienced in
starting a training-class in a local church owing

to the personalities that comprise the official group. The pastor is in danger of having to deal with personal characteristics and thereby create animosities with which he must continue to live. The plan has therefore been developed of organizing a council composed of the officers from all the churches in a city. The local ministers' conference then undertakes to do the training and appoints certain pastors to specialize in given subjects. The preliminary work having been done in this way, it is easy to start and maintain a training-class in the local church. One section of such a council would specialize in the work of deacons and deaconesses.

An isolated church would be wise to have its pastor invite a brother pastor to start the training-class in the church.

30. Association Training-class

Where churches are small and scattered it has been found wise as part of the Associational program to use one day for a series of training-classes for all church officials. One section of the instruction deals with the qualifications and duties of deacons and deaconesses.

31. Prejudice

A prejudice has arisen in many quarters against the office of deacon and deaconess. Many people refuse to accept the office after election because of this prejudice. The joke-book and the public jest have helped to produce this feeling, to the detriment of the church and those holding the office. The office of deacon and deaconess is most honorable when worthily filled, and any loyal, earnest, teachable, stewarding man or woman can fill the office with the aid of the Spirit of God and the loyal support of the people whose votes have placed him in the office.

The voice of God's people assembled after prayer and in prayerful consideration should constitute a call from God, and should overrule any prejudice that might be in the mind of any selected by the church to fill such an important Scriptural office. It is not either spiritual or in accord with common sense to refuse the call of God expressed in the prayerful vote of a Christian democracy. The fact that it is a call to a place of responsibility and opportunity ought to make acceptance most prompt.

32. The Helpful Deacon

The deacon is a much abused man. The funny column of the paper has made him the mark for an endless round of jokes and jibes which in the main are both unfair and unwise. The marvel is that there are as many good deacons as there are because the office has been belittled and the people filling it have not been given the encouragement or training to help them with their really great and responsible tasks.

All honor and help is due the earnest body of Christian men who have been willing to assume the duties of the office and do their best to help the local church. A very serious effort is needed to magnify the office and help restore every incumbent to the position intended for a deacon so that he may become more helpful to the local church life.

33. Serving Deacons

The diaconate is not an honorary post but a place of real service. A deacon or deaconess who cannot or will not serve is out of place when occupying the office unless incapacitated by long years of service or some similar good reason. In this case the incumbent should be given an honorary title, such as senior deacon or deacon emeritus, and a serving deacon should be elected to his place upon the regular board.

Recently I found a church with four deacons, three of whom were bed-ridden and the fourth man was discouraged under the load of official duties he was attempting to fulfil. This was an unfair situation for all concerned, and the Lord's work suffered seriously as a consequence. A deacon is one who serves the church, and the badge of active service should be his greatest honor and joy.

34. Business and Spirituality

Deacons are too often chosen for what is called their spirituality, and it is calmly admitted " they are not supposed to be good business men." On the contrary, the trustees are selected because they are good business men, and the statement is often made, " Oh, they can attend to the business of the church, but they are not spiritually minded." Clear thinking and a proper analysis would reveal that the business of the church must be based on spiritual foundations, and that what is good business in the life of a Christian enterprise must be eminently spiritual. The two things are in reality one and the same in a Christian life or enterprise.

35. Choosing Deacons

Deacons and deaconesses should not be chosen hurriedly, but the utmost prayer and deliberation should precede their election to this most important lay spiritual office.

Intercession should be utilized in as wide a way as possible before nominations are made. A nominating committee should be appointed more than a month before the election is to occur, and this nominating committee should give itself to much prayer. It should also consult with the pastor before making any report to the church. The reason for this is so obvious that it needs little discussion here. The deacons are the cabinet officers to work in the closest possible relationship with the chosen church leader, and they must work together in loving unity.

In my presence a short time ago a church meeting was held for the election of deacons. Nothing had been done in preparation for the election. The chairman in the open meeting called for a nomination. Instantly some one gained the recognition of the chair and placed a name in nomination. All over the room one could detect signs of disapproval, but no other nomination could be dragged out of the audience. Out of more than one hundred present about a dozen voted yea, and none voted nay, so the nominee was declared elected. The scene had interested me to such an extent that I sought an audience with the man who made the nomination. This is about what he said. " Yes, I knew the nomination would be very unpopular because the man is not fitted for the office, but he did me a good turn some time ago, so I took that method of repaying him for what he had done for me." In answer to one more question he said, " Oh, I knew that if I got the nomination in first, no one would dare nominate an opposition candidate." What a farce, and how pleasing such actions must be to the enemies of our souls and of Christ's church !

The Scripture says, " Let them first be proved."

Use prayer, deliberation, heavenly skill in choosing the deacons and deaconesses.

36. Reasons Given for Electing Deacons

A church elected a man to the office of deacon because he had lots of money and it hoped that "the honor" would open his purse in behalf of the church. If money is all that a man possesses as a qualification for the diaconate, he had better not be put in office.

A man threatened to leave the church if he was not made a deacon, "as one of my family has always held that office in this church." He was unworthy and should never have been elected.

A certain man persistently sought the office of deacon, and after three attempts to elect him had been made, some of the godly men in the church visited him to confer about his repeated attempts to capture a place in the diaconate. He finally confessed the reason for his desire was, that he might "wear a Prince Albert coat because he really looked fine in one." It was the custom in that church for the deacons to sit in the pulpit, so they wore formal dress. The one good and great reason for desiring the office of deacon is to serve God and his church.

37. A Bad Example

In a church visited recently a deacon was found whose example was a serious detriment to the local church. He was a very prosperous man, but he declined to pledge or contribute to current expenses or missions.

In another place was found a deacon who openly proclaimed that he did not believe in missions, and yet he professed to be saved under the Lord's plan of preaching the gospel to a whole lost world.

One evening in a local church, a man came into a meeting I was conducting and sat down on the front seat. He undertook to control the meeting, yet he was dirty of body and garments and so ignorant that he could not speak a correct sentence nor could he read the Bible, though he had been a deacon for seventeen years.

Four deacons out of eleven in one church said they could not pray in public, though all of them participated vigorously in a church meeting where discussion was the order of the evening.

A deacon was arrested and convicted in court for ill-treating his wife.

A deaconess was a notorious scandal-monger and broke up one home by the malicious stories she circulated.

A deaconess was notorious for her participation in dances and card-parties, but declined to do any church work on the ground that she was too busy.

These are cited as bad examples because in the long run the local church will follow the example of its lay leaders. There is great reason to be thankful that such lay officers are seldom tolerated in any local church, and further reason for gratitude that the great mass of deacons and deaconesses are high-minded stalwart Christian men and women.

38. Ordination

The call of a deacon comes from the democracy named the local church. The election if it was held under proper conditions should be the voice of God to the elected. The idea that deacons must be ordained with the laying on of hands was derived from the choosing and setting apart of the seven in Acts 6 : 1-8. We have no apostles today with their special spiritual powers. But a careful reading of that passage does not make plain that the seven thus chosen were deacons. Anyway, the laying on of the hands of a minister or other deacon does not confer special powers upon an officer, and therefore such a procedure is not essential to the formal setting apart of a deacon.

A well-planned service of recognition and instruction is a helpful occasion, as it dignifies the officer and puts him before the people with his responsibilities emphasized. Such a service should contain a charge to the church concerning the relations which must exist between the officers and the organization that called them into office. Also there should be a charge delivered by the minister to the deacons and deaconesses, in which there should be a clear statement of the general duties of their office. A prayer of consecration might also find a place in the service as well as a speech of acceptance by one of the deacons, in which could be stated an outline of the work to be done by the officers during their term of office. The whole service should produce a good atmosphere in which to work as well as dignifying or magnifying the importance of the lay spiritual office.

39. Utilizing the Deacons

The average local church needs to change its thinking about the diaconate and instead of observing deacons and deaconesses as people who are "just officials," should so carefully choose men and women of such high standards that their leadership will be followed and they will be an honor to the organization. In the life of the local church next to the pastor in influence and good works should come these officials.

40. Rotation on Duty

The practise of having two or three deacons on duty each week in order that special or routine matters may be handled promptly and in an orderly fashion, has proved itself wise in the experience of many local churches.

If there are twelve deacons, two are on duty each week, and the rotation system means that such a period of duty only comes to each individual once every six weeks.

Those on duty examine new members, give consideration to items of business that arise suddenly, and are at hand for special consultation with the pastor whenever he feels the need of such council. Matters are not handled that can be left till a regular meeting of the board of deacons.

41. Perfect People

A local church is foolish to expect to find men or women who are perfect to fill the office of deacon or deaconess.

Perfect people are in heaven where they belong and not in the membership of the local churches.

Earnest people who really love the Lord are very foolish to decline office " because they are not good enough." They will never get any better by declining opportunities to serve their Master and his people. We grow in grace by using what we have and doing our best with the endowments furnished us.

42. Church Efficiency

No local church can become truly efficient unless it possesses a trained leadership. A trained professional ministry is not sufficient for its needs, as the membership will not long continue to do what the minister teaches and does, unless the lay leaders show by their lives that they give heed to the preached Word and the example of the pastor.

A covetous deacon will set the standard of church giving far oftener than a practising pastor. A once-a-day deacon attendant upon the Sunday services is a most potent factor in the failure to produce a worshiping membership. An idle non-witnessing deacon will do much to make the church selfish and idle. No church can be efficient until the membership worship, serve, and give with due regularity. No church will produce a worshiping, serving, and giving people until the lay officers are first and foremost in the simple arts of Christian living. An efficient church is the combined result of an active, capable pastor, an intelligently selected trained body of lay leaders who by their combined powers under the leadership of the Holy Spirit train and teach all the members to fill their places in the circle of church activities.

Questions

1. What is the difference between joining an order and filling an office in a democracy?

2. Give an evidence of the divine origin of the local church.

3. Who should train the diaconate? Why?

4. Discuss the relation of prejudice to the office of deacon.

5. State the relationship between business and spirituality.

6. How should deacons be selected?

7. Discuss the ordination of deacons. Distinguish between a service of recognition and ordination.

8. What is said about perfect people?

CHAPTER III

DUTIES SUGGESTED

43. Organization

In every local church there are a great number of duties to be carried on properly. The attempt is made in this chapter to enumerate them all. But it is not the expectation that any one deacon or deaconess will be able to undertake all the varied forms of activity that are presented here, for such an expectation would be foolish. The Board of Deacons, however, should be so constituted and projected in its organization and personality that all the needed duties will be covered in an adequate way. It is plain, therefore, that a careful examination of the personalities that comprise the board will have to be made in order to accomplish the needs of the local situation through a proper assignment of each individual to one or more of the specific duties enumerated in this chapter.

44. Duties

The duties of a deacon are many in number and varied in character, but they can all be summarized under four simple heads:

(1) The care of the members of the household of faith.

(2) The oversight of the door into the church. Admission to church-membership.

(3) The charge of the door out of the church—discipline, etc.

(4) The duty of caring for the general spiritual welfare of the household as a unit.

45. Counting the Cost

To make a local church really successful the lay leaders must give a steward's portion of time to their official duties. In using the time set apart for church work the people must at least give to their efforts the same talents, acumen, business energy, and planning that they would give to a business enterprise of the highest importance.

Church work has been planned on a cheap basis, so it has been done in a slovenly, easy way, and the average results reveal it to all concerned.

Whenever the lay leaders will put a full share of their best into the church tasks, the rank and file can be brought to much greater efficiency and productivity. The rub, however, is—will they pay the great price so as to warrant a great victory.

46. Calling Upon Sick

Calling upon the sick is a very essential and helpful part of the work of a deacon and deaconess.

Gossip should be avoided. The call generally should be brief. Cheerfulness and prayer should characterize it, and when the caller leaves the room there should be left behind a spirit of love and good-will that will count for the Lord and his church. The group plan is very useful to keep track of those who are sick. Every local church should have a well-ordered ministry for sick people who are not members of the church but who are known to the membership.

Hospitals should be visited with regularity, for in them the face of need changes daily.

47. Visiting the Troubled

People in trouble should have prompt and effective ministration from the members of the household of faith. Through a group plan it should be easy for the troubled ones to be known, and then help should be given at once. In many churches there is a fellowship fund under the control of the pastor and deacons, and a wise use of such moneys is often a very great aid in meeting the needs of those in sudden trouble. Nothing will help a church more than to be known as a people who love and care for those in real need, but of course wisdom must be used in determining what measure of relief shall be proffered. To pauperize people in the name of Christ is not wise or even Christian. Personal service will often be much more effective than money help, but sometimes both money and personal ministry are essential, and then neither can be made a substitute for the other.

D

48. Church Finances

The finances of the church are a matter of supreme importance to the local organization. They are not simply a concern about money, but primarily are related to the spiritual life of the whole membership. Therefore the deacons and deaconesses must be actively related to the giving life of the church people. The finest business methods in the world will not produce a good financial condition unless first of all the membership can be produced as actively engaged in the worship life of the church. Every member should be expected to give in accordance with his God-given prosperity and with great regularity.

The deacons and deaconesses should know what every member of the church is giving in order to be able to help the covetous or ignorant to do their duty. First of all, they must be generous and regular givers themselves so that their work with others will not fail because their own lives are not visibly right with their Lord and his world cause.

Giving should be for both current expenses and missions, and a sense of discipline should be aroused so that, regardless of like or dislike, every child of God in the realms of the local church should obediently contribute to the world program of Christ.

A church recently disciplined a member because he suddenly changed his subscription to current expenses from ten dollars a week to ten cents a month. When called upon for an explanation he said that he " did not like the pastor and wanted to starve him out of his job."

49. Greeting the Strangers

Inasmuch as all of the personal ministries are within the official duties of deacons and deaconesses, the meeting and greeting of visitors and strangers should be carefully planned. It is an art to be a good host or hostess. The local church should develop that art because it will mean much to the church and to the kingdom.

To leave the greeting of visitors and strangers to the unorganized good-will of the rank and file of church-members is to have it not done or done in an ineffective way.

50. Charge of Pulpit

In the absence of the pastor the deacons should have a sense of responsibility for the ministration of the pulpit. They should meet with the visiting minister before the service in order that the details of the service may be understood by the stranger.

When the pastor is on duty he is primarily responsible for the pulpit ministrations. The deacons should not attempt to dictate to the pastor about the conduct of the service or the subject matter of sermons, but a wise pastor will keep in such close touch with his deacons that constant brotherly conferences will develop a sense of joint responsibility. A good result will then accrue to all concerned. No minister can do as he pleases regardless of the wishes of his officials and produce a good result; on the other hand no group of deacons can undertake to " boss " the minister without the results being injurious to all concerned.

51. Baptism

The ordinance of baptism is a most impressive service when properly administered. The deacons and deaconesses should see to it that the pastor has every assistance necessary to make a baptismal service attractive and symbolic.

Whenever an ordained minister can be secured he should administer the ordinance, but if a minister cannot be secured it is perfectly proper for the church to authorize a deacon to officiate under the existing emergency; but such action ought to be taken by a local church only at the time such an emergency arises. Baptism, besides being an act of obedience, is considered the door into the local church. A recently baptized convert said that the deacons were ceaselessly upon his track until he surrendered and made a profession of faith in Jesus Christ. Then came the baptismal service, and he said they swarmed around him as he went down into the baptistery but when he came up out of the water there was not one of them in sight, and they had paid no attention to him since. He said it reminded him of a verse of Scripture, namely, "And they all forsook him and fled." Baptism is counted as being the door into the church. Obedience to this ordinance by the convert should not prevent the church-members from showing the new-comer a continuous helpfulness thereafter.

52. The Lord's Supper

One of the offices of the deacons should be to serve the people attending the communion service. It is an excellent opportunity for the deacons to make an orderly and impressive occasion out of this task, but too often it is done in a slovenly manner which detracts from the solemnity of the service.

Some simple military precision is helpful in the movements of the deacons as they work among the congregation. When the pastor has handed the plates or trays to those who serve, one of them should wait till the pastor is seated, and then he should be served first of all. When the congregation has been served, the pastor in turn should wait upon the deacons after they are seated, and then the whole congregation should participate simultaneously.

A record of attendance should be noted, and a follow-up of those members frequently absent should be carefully made by the deacons and deaconesses.

The use of the individual communion service is indicated above and recommended.

53. The Prayer-meeting

The midweek service has suffered seriously in past years from non-attendance of the church-members. To secure the presence of ten per cent. of the local membership is to be an average church. The ninety per cent. of absentees suffer seriously from the lack of a developed expressional, spiritual activity. The rank and file of church-members will not respond to the appeals of the pastor and attend this service, but when the deacons and deaconesses attend and set their hearts to secure the attendance of the members the people will come in much larger numbers, and the whole life of the church will be lifted up in consequence. A good, live prayer-meeting is an essential activity in the life of any church that really is set upon the accomplishment of its tasks.

54. The Poor Fund

Many local churches have what is called a Poor Fund. The name should be changed to Fellowship Fund or some similar term.

This fund is usually committed to the care of the pastor and deacons and quite often has to be used in confidential ways in order not to hurt the feelings of people who have need of help. This fund should not depend upon an extra collection gathered after the communion service, but should be one of the items in the regular current expense fund to which every member is expected to make a weekly contribution.

55. Prayer League

When special tasks are to be undertaken, prayer leagues should be formed under the leadership of a deacon. For some weeks preceding an evangelistic campaign, an Every-member Canvass, or a Fellowship Visitation, a prayer card like that shown here should be in wide use.

INTERCESSORY PRAYER LEAGUE

With the help of the Holy Spirit I undertake to pray at least once a day for the following definite objects or people:

1. ....
2. ....
3. ....
4. ....
5. ....

Name ....

   Address ....

56. Pulpit Committee

When a new pastor is to be sought, of necessity the board of deacons should not constitute or compose the pulpit committee. One or more of them may well be appointed to serve on the pulpit committee, which should be selected in a regular way under the laws of the democracy. The reason for this is that the deacons of a local church cannot adequately represent the various component elements in the church, such as women or young people, and the pulpit committee which is seeking new leadership should be representative of the whole life of the church. A pulpit committee ought not to be too large; seven has been found to be a wise number.

57. The Family Altar

A pastor undertook to promote the cause of the family altar. By discreet inquiries he learned that only two out of nine deacons had a family altar in their homes. One morning he appeared at the house of one of his deacons at the breakfast hour, and before he left had established a family altar in that home. Soon this service had been rendered in the home of every deacon.

With their backing he then extended the campaign until a very large number of the members had adopted the plan. Many church-members have not even adopted the plan of asking a blessing at the table before beginning a meal. This is one of the matters that should be in the minds of the deacons when dealing with new-born souls who are soon to become church-members.

58. Lay Preachers

At various times in the history of the church great progress for Christ has been made by the use of lay preachers. If the church of today attempts to fulfil its mission by using only a professional ministry it is nothing short of foolish. Enough pastors and preachers cannot be produced and paid, and if this were possible it would surely develop a weakness in the church that would counteract the work done by such a ministry alone. We have Scriptural authority for the use of lay preachers in the record concerning Stephen. There seems to be a real need today of developing a large number of deacons as lay preachers, because many of them have the basic talents and there are hundreds of places where preaching is greatly needed.

59. Evangelism

The local church is one of the prime agencies for the winning of lost souls. Therefore it must have very definite plans and programs concerning evangelism, and the deacons and deaconesses must have a very particular interest in all such plans and programs. The pastor must be encouraged to use the pulpit for evangelistic ends,

Personal evangelism should be developed, and there should be classes under lay instruction for the training of personal workers.

Evangelism should spread beyond the bounds of the local field into near-by regions. It will be found that a spirit of true evangelism will help all the other concerns of the church.

60. Stewardship

Stewardship is a principle of divine origin ordained to produce a disciplined soul. It is of prime importance for a local church to produce every member as a steward, for on no other basis will the members set aside time, energy, talents, personality, and money for the Lord's work.

To be a good steward means that the whole life is a constant recognition of God's ownership of all that inheres in or belongs to it.

61. Prayer

A prayer habit must be produced in every Christian life. It will not produce itself any more than a good digestion will produce itself when a child is allowed to feed how and when he pleases. Classes on Christian living should be held under official direction.

62. Bible Reading

The habit of reading daily a portion of God's Word is vital to the development of a spiritual life. With young Christians a little help will produce a systematic reading that will be extremely valuable as the years go by.

63. Service-working

The deacons and deaconesses, under the direction of the pastor, should systematically see that every member of the church has a piece of worthwhile work to do for the Lord and his church. There is plenty of work to be done in the field of every local church, and some simple survey will reveal the tasks to be done. Then a study of the people available will enable the officials to fit together the work and the workers.

64. Worship

A worshiping people make a strong and growing church. Therefore the deacons and deaconesses should be concerned that members attend with more or less regularity upon the various services of worship in the life of the church. Without some oversight, many will neglect to attend regularly and will sooner or later be lost to the cause.

65. Study of the Bible

Every local church should plan and maintain a week-day class for the study of the Bible. A local church should establish and maintain under the leadership of the deacons a Bible readers' course. The printing in the calendar of the church of the daily passages to be read is a great help. Many churches have organized a Bible Readers' League, the object of which is to have every member read the Bible through, taking one chapter a day.

For converts or children it is not quantity of Scripture read that should be sought after, but the reading and committing to memory of one or two verses each day.

The deacons and deaconesses should be actively behind all these plans for Bible reading, and the pastor should be helping his officials in every possible manner.

66. The Group Plan

Located and designated responsibility is essential to the growth of a local church. It has been the general expectation that the minister would care for the members, but even if that was possible it would be an unwise procedure. A local church is a brotherhood, and brotherly ministrations must mark the relations of the people who compose its membership. Therefore the group plan or unit system has been found of great use. A deacon and a deaconess are paired, and to them are given about thirty-five of the members for special oversight and ministry. It is the expectation that this group will soon be devel•

oped so that they will help each other in many
ways, and in particular help every one of their
number to become regular in attendance upon
the worship life of the church, in service and in
giving.

67. Filling the Pews

One of the prime responsibilities belonging to
the diaconate is to secure a worshiping membership. A church-going people spells success.
This responsibility is often put upon the pastor,
but wrongly so, for he is to fill the pulpit and
not the pews. On the other hand, he must not
empty the pews by dreary, unprepared sermons
and a slovenly conducted service.

The first essential to a well-filled church is to
have the deacons and deaconesses in attendance.
Being present themselves, they are in a position
to urge the attendance of others. Not to attend
is to advertise the fact that they have no interest
in that department of the work. To allow the
worship life of the people to deteriorate is to destroy the real power of the local organization.

68. The Deacons' Meeting

There should be appointed a regular time and
place for the meeting of the deacons. There
is dynamic value in the formal getting together
for prayer, fellowship, and the discussion of business. In many churches a practise has grown up

of dispensing with a deacons' meeting, and the official business will be peddled over the telephone or from mouth to mouth. This leads to misunderstanding and ill-repute and should not be tolerated, or else it results in one man practically deciding the issues of the church, and that is a dangerous custom to establish in any democracy.

There should be at least a monthly session of the combined boards of deacons and deaconesses, and then the tasks confronting these officials should be assigned to the board of deacons or deaconesses, and these two groups should hold separate monthly sessions so as to check up with each other the progress or failure that has been made. At the regular sessions much prayer should be a practise, as nothing will so unify the spirit and thinking of the group as such intercession. There should be a lay chairman and a secretary for each board, and the pastor should preside at the joint monthly sessions. A careful check-up of all assigned duties should be made, and regular attendance and the fulfilment of duties accepted should be the common expectation.

Many churches now make it a rule that continued absence over a specified time constitutes a resignation from the office unless some reason accounting for the absence of the member is sent to the meetings.

69. The Lay Chairman

By right of his position as the leader of the church the pastor should be recognized as the chairman of the boards of deacons and deaconesses. No meeting of this group should ever be held without his knowledge and consent. Even when there is dissatisfaction with the minister, the policy of open conference should be used in connection with pastoral affairs.

Many pastors insist upon having the help of a lay chairman and it has been found wise to secure the appointment of such an officer. The pastor has the right to preside at all meetings when he is present, but quite often he elects not to exercise the right, and then the lay chairman conducts the meeting. In this way the pastor is training another to conduct a most important part of the church work, while at the same time he has the benefit of the counsel of a brother officer. The lay chairman, if properly chosen, will not assume the air of a " big boss " and attempt to lord it over the heritage of the Master.

70. Theology

The deacons and deaconesses should not enter into a theological discussion with converts since they are seldom equipped to carry it through. The pastor is supposed to be a trained theologian and competent to deal with the theological ques-

tions involved in a new believer's mind. If the
pastor is not competent to do this, then a pastoral change is better than to have the diaconate
muddling through the deeps of a theological discussion. On the other hand, every church-member should be able to give a reason for the hope
that is within him.

Questions

1. What are the duties of a deacon?
2. Primarily what is church financing?
3. What is the relation between pastor and
deacons in connection with the pulpit ministrations?
4. How should the Lord's Supper be conducted
in the local church?
5. Describe how a pastor promoted the family
altar.
6. What does it mean to be a good steward?
7. Discuss the group plan.
8. Who should be primarily responsible for filling the church-pews? Why?

CHAPTER IV

DEVELOPING THE MEMBERS

71. The Church-members

The church-members in a particular sense are the field of ministry for the deacons and deaconesses. No church will be really strong that neglects its membership, but any church will grow in its spiritual power when the members, under loving oversight, are trained and cultured in all the processes of a disciplined Christian life. The only hope of this being done is through the utilization of the deacons and deaconesses under the guidance of the pastor. This chapter is a comprehensive presentation of the processes to be employed in developing the membership of a local church.

72. The Household

" As we have therefore opportunity, let us do good unto all men, especially unto them who are of the household of faith " (Gal. 6 : 10).

It is a wise local church that maintains itself upon the basis of a household of faith. To be just an organization, is to be cold, formal, unloving, and more or less of a failure. To develop the household idea of Christian love and helpfulness is to make the church strong and with a great appeal to the people who witness how much " those Christians love one another."

Under the direction of the pastor, the deacons and deaconesses should pay particular attention to the members of the household of faith. To use a figure by way of illustration, the deacons and deaconesses are to act much as a father and mother acts in the home circle, but of course the element of authority differs in the church circle because it is only delegated authority and subject to strict accountability to those from whom it is derived. Unless the church-membership is properly and lovingly cared for, the whole future and also the present status of the church is endangered.

Moreover, in such a household atmosphere the deacons and deaconesses will have constant and due regard for the welfare, spiritual and financial, of the pastor. Many households are condemned in the eyes of the community by the way they treat the pastor.

73. Seeking New Members

The constant aim of the local church should be to add to its numbers " such as should be saved." All new-comers of its faith who have been related to the local churches in other places, should also be earnestly sought after.

The deacons and deaconesses should see to it that there is a constant effort being put forth to secure every prospective member that comes into the life and work of the church forces. It may well be emphasized again that it is not the expectation that the deacons and deaconesses should be doing, all the time, this particular line of work themselves, but that they shall have under their example and leadership the forces of the church doing this service as well as many other lines of activity. It is well to remember that it is much harder, but also much wiser and more resultful in the long run, to train others to do the work of the church than for a few leaders to do all they can and let the membership remain in idleness and failure.

74. Examining New Members

It is the office of the pastor to examine any one who presents himself for membership in the church so far as theological beliefs are concerned.

The pastor is supposed to be a theological specialist.

Having satisfied himself that the new-comer knows and loves the Lord Christ, the pastor should then commit the individual to the board of deacons or deaconesses. It is their task to see that before the candidate becomes a member the obligations and duties of membership in the Christian body are thoroughly understood. No one should be permitted to join the local church until he has been thoroughly instructed in all that it means to be a church-member.

Years ago in a church where I was serving, the board of deacons took their office with great seriousness. One day a young man presented himself for membership. One of the deacons read to him clause by clause the covenant of the church and secured the assent of the young man to the duty therein until it came to the presentation of the financial clause which reads " contribute cheerfully and regularly to the expenses of the local church and the work at home and abroad." The young man hastily and emphatically objected saying, " I am not going to contribute to missions, for I do not believe in them." Argument or Scripture reading was of no avail, so finally the board of deacons remanded the applicant to the care of two deacons for further instruction. The two deacons did the Lord's work well but under difficult conditions, for the young man was "mad." Prayer followed visit, and the visit was occupied by Scripture reading and prayer until after three weeks the young fellow saw the error of his way and decided that the Lord's world enterprise was part of his belief and responsibility. The candidate was then presented to the church with a recommendation from the board of deacons. For many years after he was a missionary. It would have been easier to admit him with the hope he might later change his mind, but those deacons were really filling their office.

75. Assigning Duties

Determining the availability and qualifications of the workers is a task of great importance for any local church. Let me illustrate my point by telling an experience. When a young man, one day I assigned quite hurriedly a certain important task to a splendid layman. About a week later he reported that he could not perform the work, so again in rather a hurried manner I relieved him of the first assignment and gave him another similar piece of work. That he also resigned within a week, and his action stirred up my mind considerably. So a careful study of the man's ability and adaptability was made with the help of others, with the result that when a new piece of responsibility in church finance was laid upon him he accepted it saying, "That is fine, just what I like to do." For seven years or more he did a ninety per cent. job with a most important piece of work and would qualify anywhere as a most competent treasurer and church official leader.

We need to study individuals before we assign them tasks to do.

76. Bible Reading Taught

A sinner has heard the call of God and through faith in Jesus Christ has found forgiveness and been born again.

One of the things continuously needed by a regenerated soul is the truth of God as found in the Bible. It is as essential to a spiritual life as milk is to a babe or meat to a strong man.

Every person belonging to a household of faith should be helped to develop a regular habit of Bible reading. A converts' training-class led by the deacons and deaconesses will be a great help in this particular.

Bible readings suited to the age and personal needs of the person should be in readiness for distribution. The deacons and deaconesses should visit the converts in their homes and help them to establish a family altar as well as a secret practise of Bible reading and prayer.

In a certain church the deacons have long made it a practise to visit each new member in the home. The visit proceeds after this manner:

" Have you a Bible? Will you please get it for me? Would you like me to mark a few helpful passages for you, and when you are well acquainted with all of them I will give you some more." Taking the Bible the deacon inserts a prepared marker in the following passages if the person being dealt with is a new-born soul: Psalm 1; 23; 119 : 33-40; Matthew 21 : 33-46; Isaiah; Matthew 5 : 43-48; 6 : 5-15, 19-34; 7 : 21-29; John 10 : 1-18; 12 : 20-33; Acts 2 : 37-47; 2 Corinthians 9 : 6-12; Galatians 6 : 1-9; 1 Corinthians 16 : 1, 2. If the person is an adult and has been a professor for some time, but has never learned to read the Bible, then the markers go in the Bible at the following places: Isaiah; Matthew 6 : 5-15; 7 : 13-29; 18 : 21-35; Luke 14 : 25-35; 15 : 11-32; 16 : 1-12, 19-31; Galatians 6 : 1-10; 1 Corinthians 13 : 1-13; 2 Corinthians 4 : 1-18. If the person is a child, the markers go in the following places: Psalm 23; 103 : 2; Ecclesiastes 12 : 1; Matthew 6 : 9-15; 7 : 7-12, 15-20, 24-29; 18 : 1-5; 19 : 13-15; 1 Corinthians 16 : 1, 2; 2 Corinthians 9 : 6-8; Ephesians 4 : 31, 32; 6 : 1-4; 1 John 3 : 18-24. If the child or grown person can be induced to commit to memory the passages of Scripture, the verses memorized will become some of the treasures of life. Every week or two a follow-up is maintained. This produces real results and is to be commended as a worthwhile plan.

77. Doctrines of Church Taught

Every member of a local church should know the simple truths that have brought together the group and made them voluntarily unite with each other. For instance, I am a member of a Baptist church for the following reasons:

(1) The Bible is the only and sufficient rule of faith and practise.

(2) The individual has the right to read the Bible, and under the leadership of the Holy Spirit interpret it for himself without the intervention of another.

(3) The individual has the right to worship God according to the dictates of his own conscience.

(4) The local church is to be composed only of those who give evidence that they have met Jesus in a definite surrender of their hearts and lives.

(5) Each local church is a separate body of voluntarily associated believers, and has the right within itself to determine its course of procedure according to the Word of God.

(6) Each local church has the right to associate with other similar bodies of like faith in order to do better the work of the Lord Jesus Christ.

Each year when the church school is held, a course in the doctrines should be given, using

such a book as " Baptist Beliefs," by Dr. E. Y.
Mullins.

78. Prayer Taught

Prayer is the reaching out of a soul after the
way and will of the Lord.

A prayer life must be developed just as a correct physical posture is developed. It is the result of long nurture and culture.

A prayer life must begin like the cry of a new-
born babe, as one of the first expressions of a
new-born soul. The prayer habit must be formed
like any other habit produced by a sense of love
and discipline.

Prayer consists of (1) Praise and thanksgiving
(2) Intercession, (3) Communion, (4) Asking.

Prayer should be developed in all four of these
directions. The normal, untaught development
is generally along the line of asking for what one
desires, and thus the real prayer spirit is soon
lost in selfish seeking.

Consider briefly these four prayer expressions:
(1) *Praise and Thanksgiving*. God is our Father,
and he likes to receive the praise and adoration
of his children. Moreover, it is a great aid to our
sense of reverence and our inward recognition
of his Lordship and as the Giver of every good
and perfect gift. It also produces a sense of
humility in the heart of the one who prays.

(2) *Intercession*. Intercession is prayer on be-

half of others. This is one of the noblest and most resultful of all spiritual expressions. It is one of the greatest resources of the local church and kingdom. But alas, it is used very little.

(3) *Communion.* One who prays has read the Word and remembers the admonition of the Psalmist, " Be still and know that I am God." So a child of God needs to be taught that often there is occasion to say nothing in God's presence, so that in the moments of silent communion he may speak and be heard.

(4) *Asking.* When proper attention has been given to the other three phases of prayer there is a place to make known our requests unto God for ourselves and for the things we desire for our loved ones. In untaught lives far too much time and attention is given to asking.

The posture for prayer is not a matter of supreme importance. There are times when prostration before God is the only attitude to fit the occasion. Sometimes to stand still with head bent, or to kneel, will suit the inward sense of the one who prays. Much prayer is breathed out of the soul as one walks or works.

Prayer can be private and individual. It can be public as in the prayer-meeting or at the family altar. It can be formal as part of a public service of worship.

These simple facts about prayer should be taught to every new-born child of God and also to any new members coming from other churches where the prayer life has not been produced.

A converts' training-class is one of the best methods for the deacons and deaconesses to use in teaching the prayer life and developing it among those for whom they are responsible. Some local churches plan for the deacons and deaconesses to visit the homes of all new members and there give personal help in prayer expression.

A prayer spirit is as vital to a spiritual life as movement is to a physical body.

Lay example and precedent are essential to start and maintain it among the rank and file of a local church-membership.

Here are some of the Scripture verses dealing with prayer, the use of which is commended to deacons and deaconesses: Matthew 6 : 5-15; Luke 5 : 16; John 14 : 13, 14.

79. Stewardship Taught

Stewardship is central in the teaching of God's Word because the recognition of the Lordship of Jesus Christ is essential to his Saviourhood. He cannot be Saviour without being God, and if he is God, then all that we are and have are of his creation and belong to him.

The objective of stewardship is therefore to secure from every child of God the recognition that God is the owner of all material things and personality. "Ye are not your own, ye are bought with a price." This recognition will result in the individual planning his life upon the way and will of the Lord. Also it will result in his giving to God for gospel purposes the first-fruits of all increase of time, energy, talent, personality, and money. Stewardship is mandatory in the Christian life, and it cannot be left to the voluntaryism of the individual. To emphasize this read again Luke 14 : 26-33.

Stewardship should be taught directly to every new-born soul. To leave the individual without the necessary teaching, hoping that somehow he will absorb it, is to blunt the spiritual factors of life and produce a deformed soul. Stewardship means a planned life. No life on the hit-or-miss plane can produce an adequate stewardship. God must be placed first in the plan of distribution or use of the elements of life. Stewardship involves a program in order to work out the plan. The program of a steward places in right proportion and in just distribution along the whole path of life all the elements that make it up.

Stewardship involves accountability concerning the plan and program. Without accountability failure will certainly be produced. To secure accountability we must have leadership and oversight so that the needed discipline and example will help the beginner or the weak to produce a stewardship that is honoring to the

Lord and strengthening to the believer. Deacons and deaconesses must be foremost in the exercise and promotion of stewardship.

80. Worship Attendance Taught

Attendance upon the worship services of the local church is as essential to the soul as attendance upon the dining-table is essential to the proper nourishment of the body.

A worshiping church-membership is a giving people and will also be found at work for the Lord. Any church treasurer will tell you that the people who give regularly are the people who are in constant attendance upon the various services.

Of first importance are the public services of worship on the Lord's Day. Next in importance is the prayer and testimony service during the week. New members need to be taught that attendance upon these services is not to be a matter of whim, or like and dislike of those who participate, but is to be a matter of principle because the soul needs the resultant growth.

Many churches now keep a record of the attendance of their members, and it is most helpful. With new members it is especially desirable to know that attendance is regular, and if it is not, then the deacons and deaconesses should promptly follow up the absentees. Worship is self-giving to God, and is as essential to growth in grace as the first self-giving or surrender to the Lord was essential to salvation. To come to a service of public worship just for enjoyment or to get some things you selfishly want, is to miss what worship really is. When we have really given ourselves afresh to God in all humility and repentance, then God can do in us that which is well pleasing in his sight.

81. Taught to Serve

There are some Scriptures, which I quote below, of tremendous importance to every child of God in connection with Christian service or work. "Faith without works is dead." "Work out your own salvation in fear and trembling, for so it is the good will and pleasure of God that you should do." The words of Jesus may well be added, "This do, and thou shalt live."

If the word of God is authority for our basis of Christian living then the church cannot afford to permit its membership to do as they please, but must train and discipline all to serve in such ways as will allow them to do their best for the Lord and his cause.

There is a task for every one, and every one should be carefully studied by the leaders so that they may be given the right sort of work to do. In illustrating the need of care in this direction, I remember a deacon to whom I assigned a certain duty. In a month or so he came and said

"Pastor, I cannot make a success of that piece of work." So rather petulantly I gave him some other duty, but within a week he returned to say that he was very sorry but he was not fitted to do the thing assigned him. Aroused, I spent some time in studying the man and then I assigned him a duty of dealing with a large group of children, and for many years he was a joy and blessing to his pastor and the local church.

People will do well the things they like to do and for which they are best adapted, and the tasks of the church are so varied that the work of the church should be so planned that every one is utilized in his proper place.

Having assigned the member a task, the officials or leaders should see that proper help is given the individual so that the task is understood, the methods to be used plain, and the personal relations with coworkers pleasant. The deacons and deaconesses should conduct training-classes for various workers such as personal workers in evangelism, teacher-training classes for teachers, and visitors-coaching conferences for every-member canvasses and fellowship visitations.

82. Organizing Groups

Groups of individuals who have similar tastes, ambitions, or work should be organized into leagues or circles in order to help each other attain their objective. With each such league or circle should be associated some of the lay leaders in order that they may encourage and stimulate the effort of the group. The organization of the circle or league should be in as simple a form as is possible. Regular but infrequent group meetings should occur. Prayer leagues for intercession have very great value. A stewardship league with a tithers' band can be made a most effective instrument, and will help to increase the productivity of individual Christian lives. Evangelistic bands are very useful in any local church. Such group organizations will not prosper or be long maintained unless the deacons and deaconesses, as lay officials, are interested and enlisted in their behalf.

Questions

1. What is said about a household of faith?

2. Who should examine new members? How should it be done?

3. Discuss the relation of deacons to a Bible-reading membership.

4. State six basic principles of a local Baptist church-member.

5. What are the four phases of prayer? Discuss them.

6. Describe the objectives of stewardship.

7. What is said about worship attendance?

8. Why is some form of serving essential to Christian living?

CHAPTER V

CHURCH DISCIPLINE

83. Discipline

" Go ye therefore, and disciple all nations."
To disciple is to discipline, and it is done under
the power of the Holy Spirit by applying the
Word of the Lord to the hearts and lives of
people.

After regeneration has taken place, discipline
proceeds as truth is taken into the heart and the
life in all its varied activities assimilates the truth
and lives under its power. The local church, by
varied processes and under trained lay leaders,
must produce a disciplined body of believers.

There is another form of discipline which con-

F

sists of measures calculated to punish offenders, but the church has very little need of such punitive discipline when it has properly carried out the purpose of Christ in making disciples upon his basis of truth.

84. Disciplinary Spirit

Any exercise of discipline in the local church must be tempered with the Bible injunction, "Consider thyself lest thou also be tempted." On the other hand, the very personal knowledge of one's own dangers and weakness should create a strong desire to help every one escape the evil results of failure and weakness. Deacons and deaconesses in guiding the disciplinary spirit of a local church must not be animated by an attitude of overlordship or be moved to action by anger or vengeance. The last use that should be made of church discipline is to punish, but constant use should be made of it to correct the tendency to failure.

The average local church has lost entirely the disciplinary spirit, and in an atmosphere of cowardice allows its members to do as they please until all signs of Christian life have disappeared in the experiences of many a church-member, and then in a quiet way a certain block of names is removed from the roll of the church. Such a process is disgraceful because it is a well-known fact that most of the people concerned in such an erasure of names from the roll could have been saved if loving brotherly and sisterly methods had been applied in the early stages of delinquency. We must in all love and honor create a spirit of discipline in the local church, and this will never be done until the deacons and deaconesses measure up to their responsibilities and opportunities.

85. Nurture and Culture

Discipline cannot be produced in any group at a moment's notice. It is a thing of slow development and is largely a product of leadership and example.

An army is not a great mass of loosely-related men, but is the result of the steady increase of a sense of interdependence and accountability in a large number of individuals. To produce these factors intensive and continuous application is required from experienced and trained leaders. Under processes of nurture and culture an army grows out of a mob of men. The church will be a mob until such processes are used in connection with the individuals that voluntarily relate themselves to that body. Nurture and culture are both quite costly processes and take considerable time as well as effort to produce real results. Nurture and culture are twin processes, one working from the inside, the other applied from the outside. To be effective, these two factors cannot be developed or applied in a hit-or-miss manner, but they must come into the life as a result of scientific processes. The need is for men and women trained to do a scientific piece of nurture and culture with every one who joins a local church. The minister cannot do it. In many pastorates it would be a physical impossibility. He is one among many, and if he could do it, it would not be wise for him to do it alone.

Lay leaders must be produced to do such work, for then it will be effective with the membership and at the same time will develop a corps of trained lay officials that will constitute a permanent strength to the local church.

86. Endure to the End

When an individual makes a profession of faith in Jesus Christ and then unites with the church, the goal has not been reached. Only a start in the individual Christian life has been made. The goal of the church is to take a regenerated soul and through the ministry of the Spirit and the Word nurture and culture this spiritual babe so that through cooperative worship, service, and stewardship a strong matured soul shall come to the end of this earthly pilgrimage ready to meet the Lord and Master. The local church must impress itself afresh with the seriousness of its task, which is to help people bear fruit in their lives and to " endure unto the end." Scripture says, " He that shall endure to the end, the same shall be saved " (Mark 13 : 13).

87. Dismissing Members

In dismissing members from one local church to another there are several things that the deacons and deaconesses need to keep in mind.

First of all, there is the honor and integrity of the church which is granting a letter of dismission. To say that a member is in good and regular standing is an easy thing, but is it true? If it is true, well and good, but if it is not a statement of fact, then it is misrepresentation and a lie. What reflex influence will such conduct have upon the lives of the other members. To say, " Well, there are no charges pending against the brother," is to beg the question and avoid the issue. If the reader should rob a jewelry store tonight, he is a robber even if the sheriff does not prefer a charge against him. A church should make it a point to tell the truth in love about a member when dismissing him, and the very fact that such is the practise of the church will help to maintain a worth-while standard in the life of the church. A good " Letter of Dismission " form will be found in " A Manual of Church Methods."

Next, let us consider the reflex action upon the member to be dismissed when it is well known that a blank form of letter is used that

disguises the truth about a good member and
outrages the truth about an unfaithful member.
The whole process is a farce and breaks down
the value of resultful expectation and a disciplined standard of living. The good member
should be passed on for his real value to the
cause, while the non-participating, troublesome
member should be passed on in such a manner
as to promote his highest interests as well as the
interests of the Lord's cause. Many a church
has gleefully dismissed a trouble-maker to another church, well knowing that it was passing
trouble on to a sister church, and the result is
often to confirm the breeder of church troubles
in his dangerous habits. To tell the truth in love
would be a warning to the person that his bad
habits were known and would be dealt with
promptly. Last of all, consider the wrong done
to the church which is to receive a delinquent
person without knowing the facts about the individual. If the receiving church knew the facts
and was really on its job, certain things would be
done before the delinquent person was received,
and the state of transition from one church to
another would be used to start a weak or way-
ward soul on a new course compatible with the
requirements of membership. In this way deacons and deaconesses would have a real opportunity to help many souls to realize just what
church-membership means. Of course, the

church letter would be made out by competent
and fair officials in the dismissing church and
sent direct to the pastor of the receiving church,
and only the officials would know its contents.
A letter of dismission ought never to be delivered
to the person but sent from a church to a church.

One thing needs to be noted here. Often I am
told this plan would not work and officials could
not be trusted to keep secret the contents of such
letters. Hundreds of churches have been using
such a letter form, and as I mingle among them
no complaint has ever come to me that the diaconate divulged the contents of such letters they
had received. It will work and to the advantage
of all concerned.

88. The Processes of Discipline

Every local church needs to possess such a sense
of household discipline as is found in a well-regu-
lated home. In such a home love abounds. Where
love abounds authority is not a thing of fear, but
of tender recognition of love. Consequently, authority is exercised promptly for the good of all
concerned. Discipline should proceed in this
manner in a local church. The brotherly love
of the household should keep constant watch
upon all the membership in order to be helpful
as soon as possible. When a weakness develops
in an individual, loving personal help should
promptly be given by those best able to give it.

This will involve intercession and personal visitation. It may involve helping to form new habits of public and private worship, or to advance lines of personal stewardship. The aid of the deacons or deaconesses should be sought if the help thus given by a brother or sister is not soon resultful. The officials with their wider experience will then put further loving helpfulness and teaching into action. The aid of the pastor will be sought. Under the power of the Holy Spirit such disciplinary processes will be mightily effective in most cases.

Suppose, however, a member refuses, we will say, to attend the house of worship, or declines to participate in a reasonable way in the fraternal ministries of the household of faith, or refuses to give of his substances for the support of a gospel ministry at home and abroad; then a further disciplinary process is needed. How shall it proceed? First, the individual must be taught the will and way of the Lord of his salvation. Then, in love, the obligations assumed when church-membership was voluntarily sought, must be made plain. Intercession for the individual must be planned, and prayer with him must be held constantly. Patient continuance in such a course must be exhibited by the deacons or deaconesses handling the case; but, finally, if every evidence shows that the individual is not attempting to follow Christ and is not in fellowship with the purposes of the church, then he is cited to appear before the board of deacons. A prayerful, loving spirit must characterize the interview, but if it ends without a new purpose in the heart and life of the individual, then the board of deacons should recommend to the church that the hand of fellowship should be withdrawn and the individual excluded. At such a church session the person implicated is lovingly given every opportunity to defend his course of action. Where a member is personally implicated in crime, the same procedure should obtain, but exclusion should not result *in any case* when repentance and a new course of life are brought about. Under such circumstances if the repentant one is a church official he should resign his offices.

The act of exclusion should not end the relations of the church with the delinquent, but a ministry should be promptly instituted with the object of seeking the redemption of the lost one and his restoration to fellowship.

Discipline of this character is essential to the welfare of any local church. To fail in the exercise of such loving processes is to condemn the church to weakness and failure.

Discipline of this character can only be exercised when the spiritual life of the church is of such a high character that the unity of the household is assured, no matter who may be the subject of discipline.

89. The Church Covenant

Such a church covenant as is given here is used by the local church to summarize the membership objectives or, in other words, to express the united aims of the body. The deacons should read it to every incoming member. It then becomes mandatory because of their own free will all who join have expressed their determination to seek the objectives thus set forth. A sample covenant is given here:

CHURCH COVENANT

Having been influenced by the Holy Spirit, as we humbly trust, to turn from our sins and to receive Jesus as our Lord and Saviour; and on profession of our faith in him, having been baptized into the name of the Father, Son, and Holy Spirit, we do covenant and agree together that we will walk, by the help of God, in all the commandments of our Lord Jesus Christ.

Furthermore, we promise that we will watch over and counsel one another in the spirit of brotherly love, that we will remember one another in our prayers, and that we will aid one another in sickness and distress.

We further agree that, as we have opportunity, we will do good unto all men; that we will strive to win our kindred and acquaintance to the Saviour and to spread the gospel to every nation; that we will give as God has prospered us for the support of the gospel ministry abroad and in our midst, and for the expenses of the church, and for the relief of the poor; that we will bring up such as may be under our care in the nurture and admonition of the Lord; that we will not forsake the assembling of ourselves together, but as far as possible we will attend all the meetings of the church; that we will loyally uphold the authority of the church in all things save in matters of conscience; that we will strive to promote the prosperity, spirituality, and unity of the church, and to sustain its ordinances, doctrines, and discipline.

We further covenant that we will maintain secret prayer; that we will live carefully in this present world and will abstain from everything that will cause our brother to stumble or that will bring reproach upon the cause of Christ; that we will strive to grow in the grace and knowledge of our Lord and Saviour; that we will give ourselves soul and body and all that we have into God's hand, to be kept and used by him as seemeth good in his sight; that through life amidst evil and good report we will humbly and earnestly seek to live to the honor and glory of him who loved us and gave himself for us.

Name ....

Date ....

90. Stewarding Deacons

Deacons and deaconesses should be actively participating as stewards in the local church. This simply means that, under the plan of salvation, they must recognize the Lordship of Christ and utilize some of their time, energy, talents, personality, and substance so that God will have his first and dynamic share of all that inheres in or belongs to the individual life. A program should therefore be made so that there will be separated time and energy as well as separated money for use in Christian services.

A hit-and-miss life will be a failure, but a plan and program engaged in by a steward will lead to accomplishments and richness of soul and mind. To do this stewarding will require a real sense of discipline under the grace of the Lord Christ, but when done by the deacons it will spread rapidly through the church and engage other lives in an effective stewardship.

91. The Church Trouble-maker

The apostle Paul evidently knew something about the trouble-maker in the local church for he wrote as follows to the church at Rome:

Now I beseech you, brethren, mark them which cause divisions and offenses contrary to the doctrine which ye have learned; and avoid them. For they that are such serve not our Lord Jesus Christ, but their own belly; and by good words and fair speeches deceive the hearts of the simple (Rom. 16 : 17, 18).

To accomplish its task, the local church must be united so that when an individual or a small group arise to cause divisions and offenses they should be avoided; in other words, if they cannot be changed in their course they should be excluded from the fellowship.

In doing this the deacons must first lovingly deal with the offenders, and then report the case to the church if disciplinary action is finally necessary.

92. Giving and Living

There is far too much hesitation in the local church to pursue the matter of finances. Fear seems to possess the minds of both the ministry and the lay leaders. The teachings of Scripture on this subject are not known or else they are avoided. This is indicated by the loose manner in which such matters have been handled, and this fear and looseness have produced trouble. However much work and prayer are involved in the new methods, much more trouble is caused by the old inadequate, improper method of conducting the money affairs of a church. Lay officers must assume the brunt of the personal side of the campaign to produce every member of the church as an adequate, systematic, joyful giver. Giving must not be left to the voluntary spirit of the people, but it is a mandatory concern of the lay spiritual officers. The pastor, if he is wise, will give his deacons and deaconesses every possible support as they undertake to produce a giving people. To give is to live spiritually, while not to participate properly in the giving life of the church is to condemn oneself to a slow spiritual death.

93. Covetousness

The sin of covetousness is a most prevalent one, and the church has not helped greatly to cure it, but until within recent years has rather condoned it. Church after church presents the spectacle of half the members giving nothing of record for any gospel purpose through the local church, and too often the practise cannot be broken up because some of the leading officials are among the delinquents. Covetousness is most serious because in essence it is idolatry. The person loves a thing more than God, so refuses to give to God the first-fruits of all the increase despite the command of his Lord that he must give. Too often sheer cowardice is behind the failure of the church to cure covetousness. It can be cured, it has been cured in hundreds of local churches within the past several years. In such churches where almost all the members are contributors of record, there is far less trouble than where covetousness is allowed to reign unmolested. This matter vitally concerns the deacons and deaconesses, because too often the sin has a good lodgment in that official group, and an effective campaign must start with the leaders.

94. Gossip and Small Talk

Every church officer should avoid small talk and gossip as it is the cause of much weakness in the local church. This should be particularly true of the deacons and deaconesses, who are often called upon to hear officially things that should be securely locked in the secret recesses of their minds. Talk up a pastor, and avoid allowing people to talk him down to you. Pass on good things and helpful facts about people and their work, while in love and secrecy keep the things known about people that are disagreeable and injurious, and then see to it that they are handled so as to cure them of their injurious possibilities.

When gossip and small talk prevail in a local church, it indicates a lack of Christian discipline.

Questions

1. What is the relation between disciple and discipline?

2. What is the relation between nurture and culture?

3. Discuss dismissing members.

4. Describe the processes of discipline.

5. What is a church covenant?

6. What five elements of life are concerned with stewardship?

7. Quote Romans 16 : 17, 18

8. What is covetousness?

CHAPTER VI

SOME RELATED TOPICS

95. Related Topics

The contents of this chapter may not be specifically related to the office of deacon or deaconess, but are included here because the topics considered have been found of value in discussing with such officers the general productivity of the local church in its many lines of activity.

In many cases a local church is weakened by a little misunderstanding or some slight lack of coordination or some failure to secure a right process, and it is to help the deacons and deaconesses in their official relations that these general topics have been formed for presentation into a separate chapter.

96. The Local Church—Its Purpose

The purpose of the local church is to allow the children of God under the leadership of the Holy Spirit to cooperate with each other in an adequate way, so that all may grow in grace and the knowledge of their Lord through the processes of an intelligent evangelism which covers in its phases of activity the whole world.

This purpose can never be fulfilled when a church hires a minister to do the work of the church, and then the members do or do not as seems well to their selfish moods. The purpose can only be fulfilled when such an organization is perfected under the teaching and preaching of the minister, which will produce a cooperating people grouped under lay leadership so as to allow all to be developed in service. Hence the Scriptural lay office of deacon and deaconess to be filled by men and women proved fit for their tasks.

G

97. The Kingdom—The Local Church

Not every member of the local church belongs to the kingdom of God, because some have crept into the church without being regenerated. It is also true that not every one who belongs to the kingdom of God has found a place in the local churches, though every child of God should seek membership in the church because Scripture makes plain the fact that under the direction of the Holy Spirit the church was established and is maintained. A paid and professional ministry without lay assistance cannot take proper oversight of the regenerated to get them all into the church and then give them adequate oversight in order to keep them in proper relations to the divine institution. Therefore the offices of deacon and deaconess were provided so that there might be proper correlation between the members of the kingdom and the membership of the local church.

98. An Official View-point

A long official tenure is apt to produce an official consciousness and view-point that is not to the best interests of a Christian democracy. A small group of people constantly together are in the long run liable to lose touch with the inherent needs and view-points of a larger outside group. It is a constant experience of the writer to go into local churches and find the officiary quite content to muddle along in the rut and on the verge of a real failure, while in the mass of the membership is to be found a desire for progress and modern methods in order to meet the situation confronting the organization. But the mass is powerless under the manipulating hand of the official group. Too often this situation leads to controversy and a split church. A deacon should not be permitted to hold his office continuously so that he loses his representative capacity and urges his own will and desire rather than the will of the body he represents and their desire to do the biggest possible thing for the Lord and his church.

After three or five years in office, it is very helpful for a deacon to retire for a year and mingle again in unofficial circles, and so learn the heart's desire and view-point of the great mass of the church-members.

99. Church Bosses

A board of deacons should never be allowed to control the church as if they were its bosses. They are the servants of the church for Christ's sake, and their main objective should be to develop a body of people capable of handling to the best possible advantage all the concerns of the church. Instead of assembling power in their own hands the deacons should constantly be producing other individuals to whom should be committed the duties and powers of the church. In some churches one finds the board of deacons in absolute and final control of the affairs of the church, and this without any constitutional right. This is unwise both for the officials concerned and also for the church because it virtually destroys the democracy of the body and fails to produce a developed and participating people. Strong wise men in Christian churches do not become bosses but are real leaders producing a constituency with a sense of divine responsibility and human opportunity. The boss is a curse in the political realm but in the church he is one of the most destructive forces to be found fighting against the purposes for which the local church was constituted. "And if a man also strive for masteries, yet is he not crowned, except he strive lawfully. The husbandman that laboreth must be first partaker of the fruits" (2 Tim. 2 : 5, 6).

100. Senior Deacons

In a local church some time ago, I found a board of deacons composed of four men, three of whom were too feeble to get out of the houses they lived in. In consequence the church was seriously handicapped because the by-laws provided for only four deacons, and not for worlds would they depart from their time-worn custom.

The proposal was made that the three incapacitated men be made senior deacons for life, and then three new active men be chosen to fill the office of deacon. A senior deacon under such circumstances is entitled to all the honors of the office, but is not assigned to the tasks of the diaconate. Such a senior deacon is sometimes called deacon emeritus.

101. Charge of Prayer-meeting

In the absence of the pastor the deacons should have a real sense of responsibility for the conduct and success of the midweek or prayer service.

A wise pastor will plan with his board of deacons who should be appointed to lead the meeting. It need not necessarily be one of the deacons. No offense should ever be taken by any deacon when some other competent person is put into service, for the highest type of efficiency is not alone in the ability to do things oneself but in developing and utilizing others to fulfil the needed church functions. In an emergency, when no plan has been made by the pastor, the board of deacons automatically assumes charge of the prayer service.

102. Many Offices

Quite frequently in a local church there is to be found one or more individuals holding many offices throughout the various departments. In one case a man was found who held nine official positions. It is needless to say that he did not fulfil the requirements of those offices, but he did keep others from opportunities for service, which is a pernicious result. Unless it is an exceptional case, the rule should be one office to an individual. If a deacon or deaconess really meets the requirements of that great lay responsibility, it will require all the time, energy, and talent which any individual can give out of an ordinarily busy life while at the same time fulfilling the needs of personal spiritual culture. It is much better to do a one hundred per cent. job in one office than to do a thirty per cent. job in three positions.

103. Every-member Visitation

No finer method has ever been developed for cultivating the prayer and visitation spirit in a congregation than the Every-member Fellowship Visitation. Financial goals should not be introduced into the objectives of such a visitation. On a Sunday afternoon, under the leadership of the deacons and deaconesses, teams of two men or women carefully chosen many weeks in advance should call upon every member in their homes. Church goals, talking up the pastor, enlistment for service, and perhaps enrolling pupils for a church school should be the

main topics of discussion. Prayer should be of
fered in every home visited, but it ought not to
be formal stilted prayer but a real spirit of intercession giving expression to itself. The
visitors should go in pairs, and the calls each
pair is to make should be assigned to them
after very careful selection. The aim is to create
enthusiasm, unify the fellowship, and learn the
needs of the membership so that the deacons and
deaconesses will have exact information about
every one on which to base their plans for future
ministries.

104. Every-member Canvass

As a piece of spiritual ministry among the
church-membership in order properly to produce
the needed church finances an Every-member
Canvass cannot be surpassed.

Briefly the canvass is conducted in the following manner. There is a period of intercession for
all non-contributors and those avoiding an adequate share of the finances of the church. Then
the budget of expense is made up and presented
to the church. Canvassers are enlisted, and they
as well as the whole church are educated as to the
needs of the situation locally and around the
world. A day for the canvass is appointed and
carefully prepared for. On the day of the canvass a high tide of spiritual enthusiasm should
have been attained, and God's people with love

and joy provide the pledges which will produce week by week all the money that is needed to care for the obligations of the local church as well as for the missionary work around the world. The deacons and deaconesses should be particularly interested and enthusiastic about the canvass, for it means a real revival of religion each year when it is properly done.

105. A Membership Record

Every church should make up a very careful record of the membership roll. Here is a sample record card:

Name .... Group ....
Address .... Phone ....
School or Business ....
Member of Church .... Life Plan ....
Religious Interest ....
Chief Interest ....
Remarks ....
Deacon .... Year ....

106. Enlistment Card

A card similar to that shown here is now used by many churches when receiving new members. Such churches make it necessary for the applicant to sign up before they are eligible to be presented to the congregation for action. The deacons present the enlistment card to the new-comer.

BAPTIST CHURCH, CALIFORNIA

ENLISTMENT CARD

It is my earnest purpose, upon becoming a member of the —— Church, to aid, in every reasonable way I can, the successful carrying out of its program. To this end—

First—I shall make it my practise to be a regular attendant at the following Church services (Check the ones you have in mind) :

Morning Service .... Prayer Meeting .... Y. P. U. ....

Evening Service .... Bible School .... Women's Union ....

Second—I shall be willing to serve in any capacity connected with the Church organization for which I am at all fitted. I should prefer to work in one of the capacities which I have marked on the organization chart with V (see back of card). I have had training and experience in the capacities I have marked with X.

Third—As a good steward of God, I hereby agree to contribute through the treasuries of the —— Church—

For Current Expenses, the sum of $.................

For World-Wide Missions, the sum of $.................

Foundation Fund $.................

Name ....

Address .... Phone ....

ORGANIZATION CHART

GENERAL CHURCH WORK

....Deacon
....Deaconess
....Trustee
....Clerk
....Treasurer
....Beneficence Treasurer
....Usher
....Music Committee

....Clerical Work
....Singing in the Choir
....Junior Church Work
....Visiting
....Publicity
....Playing Piano
....Playing other instrument

BIBLE SCHOOL

Teaching—
....Regular
....Substitute
Teacher-Training—
....Teacher
....Student

Service in—
....Boys' Work
....Girls' Work
....Home Department

....Cradle Roll Dept.
....Children's Herald and
        World Crusade
Official Work—
....Superintendent
....Asst. Superintendent
....Departmental Supt.
....Secretary
....Treasurer
....Enrolment Secretary
....Social Secretary

MEN'S BROTHERHOOD

....Attend the monthly
    meetings

....Serve as officer

WOMAN'S SOCIETY

Official Work—

....President
....Vice-president
....Recording Secretary
....Corresponding Secretary
....Treasurer
....Circle President

Committees—
....City Missions
....Programs
....Social Courtesy
....Floral Decorations
....Work Department
....Nursery
....Literature
....White Cross
....Commissary

GIRLS' WORK

....World Wide Guild   ....Corner Club

YOUNG PEOPLE'S WORK

....Senior Y. P. U.   ....Junior
....Intermediate

—— CHURCH, CALIFORNIA

In recognition of the foregoing we, the members of the —— Church, covenant, on our part, to do all within our power to aid .... in carrying out the purpose to which .... has subscribed.

Signed on behalf of the Church,

...., Deacon

...., Clerk

COVENANT

Having been led, as we believe, by the Spirit of God, to receive the Lord Jesus Christ as our Saviour, and, on the profession of our faith, having been baptized in the name of the Father, and of the Son, and of the Holy Spirit, we do now, in the presence of God and this assembly, most solemnly and joyfully enter into Covenant with one another as one body in Christ.

We engage, therefore, by the aid of the Holy Spirit, to walk together in Christian love; to strive for the advancement of this Church in knowledge, holiness, and comfort; to promote its prosperity and spirituality; to sustain its worship, ordinances, discipline, and doctrines; to contribute cheerfully and regularly to the support of the ministry, the expenses of the Church, the relief of the poor, and the spread of the gospel through all nations.

We also engage to maintain family and secret devotion; to religiously educate our children; to seek the salvation of our kindred and acquaintances; to walk circumspectly in the world; to be just in our dealings, faithful in our engagements, and exemplary in our deportment; to avoid all tattling, backbiting, and excessive anger; to abstain from the sale and use of intoxicating drinks as a beverage; and to be zealous in our efforts to advance the kingdom of our Saviour.

We further engage to watch over one another in brotherly love; to remember each other in prayer; to aid each other in sickness and distress; to cultivate Christian sympathy in feeling and courtesy in speech; to be slow to take offense, but always ready for reconciliation, and mindful of the rules of our Saviour to secure it without delay.

We moreover engage that when we remove from this place we will, as soon as possible, unite with some other Church where we can carry out the spirit of this Covenant and the principles of God's word.

Sign Here ....

READ CAREFULLY AND PRESERVE

107. Stewardship Pledge

It has been found wise to circulate quite constantly in all departments of the church a stewardship pledge with a tithers' enlistment attached to it. One of the deacons should cooperate with the financial officers in this matter. A sample card is shown here:

THE LEAGUE OF CHRISTIAN STEWARDS

I desire to enroll in " The League of Christian Stewards." I recognize that I am a steward of my life, my time, and my money. I agree to give to the work of the kingdom a just proportion of my personal time and influence and to set apart a definite proportion, at least one-tenth, of my income to be used for the advancement of the kingdom of our Lord throughout the world and for the furthering of the interests of my own church.

Name ....

Street .... City ....

State............. Church............ Date...........

This card should be kept on file in the local church. Every six months the person in charge of stewardship in the local church should send to the State headquarters the number of those who have been enrolled since the last report. The State office will send to the person so reporting literature for distribution in the church.

108. Making Enemies

Many, many times the local churches fail because of fear. Church officers avoid discipline because they fear family, relatives, and friends. Financial follow-ups are not made because there is fear that some one will be made angry. Sometimes the pulpit is silent because there is a fear that offense will be taken at plain speaking. Perfect love casteth out fear, and in the brotherly love of the church fellowship we should even dare to make enemies if it is necessary to help the household to higher standards of Christian living. Often when love ruled, it was found that the fears were groundless, and friends were made by doing right instead of enemies as was feared.

109. Salvation

The process of individual salvation has two phases, God's side and ours. That it may be real and permanent, both parties must have fulfilled all the requirements. Salvation is well started on its wonderful course by the divine act of regeneration, but it comes to its eternal goal only as the regeneration is proved by the fruitage of the new-born soul. "By their fruits ye shall know them."

Salvation is to be received from the Lord without money and without price, it is free to all, but the proof that it has really been received is found in the immediate assumption of all its tremendous costs. If you have really received salvation, it will become the most costly thing in all your life and activity. To cheapen salvation or to try to make it easy is to destroy its value.

110. Expectation

The members of a local church can, in the main, do as they please, because the psychology of their situation is that there has never been created any expectation that they will even do the things they solemnly covenanted to do when they united with the church. In many cases the situation is even worse than that, for the member when joining was not even confronted with the obligations of membership, but was allowed to unite as if he was incurring no responsibility whatever. A lack of expectation inevitably induces a failure to produce. Common sense and good psychology lay down a very definite expectation and then proceed to build a plan and a program that aims to help every one concerned produce the needed result.

Recently in a church I found a church treasurer who had not been in the church building for seven years. A man living next door to the same church, though the richest man in town, had not made a contribution for ten years nor had he been to a service of worship, yet he was in good and regular standing and was granted a letter so stating. Such lack of expectation is nothing short of criminal and leads to standards of living that make Christianity a farce and the Christian profession a lie. Every church should maintain a minimum standard of expectation.

111. Democracy

Education is the motive-power of democracy. An intelligent, trained people will follow the right type of leadership, but the right type of leadership must be highly trained after being carefully chosen.

No democracy, least of all the local church, can afford to delegate authority to officers who are ignorant of their responsibility and untrained in the performance of their tasks.

The church democracy can be transformed whenever its diaconate, having been properly chosen, is then properly educated.

112. Machinery

Machinery and methods are good in their place, but in the local church they must never be allowed to dim the importance of personal service and spiritual dynamic. Observation of church life over a very wide area would cause me to say that quite often the diaconate are giving far too much time and attention to the machinery and methods of the church, and in consequence are not paying nearly enough attention to persons and spiritual dynamic. My understanding and experience causes me, therefore, to point out that if the local church is to be strengthened and made more effective, the lay spiritual officers must hereafter devote themselves to a real spiritual ministry among the church-members, and other officers must quite largely take care of machinery and methods.

113. The Final Word

Many details have been presented here. All of them concern methods that are in use in many churches. Not all of them can be found in any one church. Not any of the methods indicated herein are pure idealism, but every one of them is practical even if it does partake of idealism. The aim of the leaders of every church should be to get acquainted with as many methods as possible, and then with full knowledge of the local situation select those ways and means for their church that will produce it as a first-rate organization. One final caution needs to be given here. Because some leader reports that a certain method failed in some other local churches, is no reason why it should not be tried elsewhere provided it aims in the direction of some known need, but it may be wise to make some modifications. It is better to give it a good honest trial than to go on without any attempt to better a failing situation. Leadership is of supreme importance in the life of a local church, and the right kind of leadership will not miss any good thing that will help the cause of the Lord in their local church.

114. Bibliography

Church Officers at Work, G. H. Asquith
A Short Baptist Manual of Policy and Practice, N. H. Maring and W. S. Hudson
The Church Business Meeting, R. D. Merrill
Baptist Beliefs, E. Y. Mullins
A History of the Baptists, R. G. Torbet

Questions

1. What is the purpose of the local church?

2. Distinguish between the kingdom and the local church.

3. What is said about an official view-point?

4. Discuss democracy and a church boss.

5. Why should only one office be held by an individual member?

6. What is the difference between an Every-member Visitation and an Every-member Canvass?

7. What three points are presented to an incoming member by the Enlistment Card?

8. What is said about salvation?

GENERAL TOPICAL INDEX

GENERAL TOPICAL INDEX

(The figures refer to the paragraphs which are numbered consecutively through the book.)